INVADE MY PRIVACY

INVADE
MY PRIVACY

Fran Landesman

THE PERMANENT PRESS
RD 2, Noyac Road
Sag Harbor, N.Y. 11963

First Publication 1978 in Great Britain by
Jonathan Cape Ltd.

First publication in the United States 1984 by
The Permanent Press, RD2 Noyac Rd., Sag Harbor,
New York

Library of Congress Catalogue Number: 83-063244
International Standard Book Numbers: 0-932966-44-6

Printed in the United States of America

To *both* my publishers

Contents

CRIES FROM THE HEART

Invade My Privacy

I wish you would invade my privacy
Scatter my silence
Mess up my day
I wish you'd leave your mark all over me
Handle my secrets
Teach me to play
I wish you would

I want you to assault my mystery
Open my letters
Finger my face
I want you to invade my privacy
Use up my hours
Fill up my space
I want you to

I'm so sick of living in dreams
With music and books for friends
So safe in my ivory tower
Improving the cloudy hour
With intimate odds and ends

I want someone to see inside of me
Fondle my fancies
Enter my art
I wish you'd penetrate my privacy
Conquer my vanity
Touch my heart

Somewhere Called Home

Sing softly, sing sadly
Of somewhere called home
A town by a river
All muddy and brown
It wasn't so lovely
It wasn't so kind
But now I'm so lonely
It glows in my mind
The winters were bitter
The summers were fierce
But life offered something
That seemed like a choice

Sing softly, sing sadly
Of something called youth
Of music that moved us
And seemed like the truth
The trumpets still echo
In rooms far away
I learn a new language
To curse a new day
But I am a stranger
Wherever I roam
Sing softly, sing sadly
Of somewhere called home

I Should Have Been Dancing

I wasted my whole life
Messing up yours
When I should have been dancing
I was slamming the doors

I sulked in the spotlight
Wearing a frown
When I should have been dancing
I was putting you down

We could have been sensational
A couple of luminous stars
Could have been inspirational
When all the tomorrows were ours

I gave you a hard time
Fighting our wars
When I should have been dancing
I was settling scores
When I should have been making sense of my life
I was busy messing up yours

Through the Smoke

Though I see your lips are moving
I can't hear you through the smoke
But I wouldn't say I'm losing
I could use another toke

We've been up all night unwinding
With some nice refreshing coke
And the room is pretty funky
I can't hear you through the smoke

But I know you're out there somewhere
I can spot your silhouette
And I know you're gonna need me
Though you're playing hard to get

We are all a little crazy
Just some old R. Crumb cartoons
And when all the games are over
We will lick each other's wounds

Now your fingers touch my teardrops
I've been crying at a joke
I can see you through the music
I can hear you through the smoke

After Many a Summer

In the morning grass the dew is gleaming
Picnics for a dragon and a faun
Later come the coffins and the candles
After many a summer dies the swan

We may have some sunny days to sing of
Nights of love that lasted till the dawn
Still behind it all remains the echo
After many a summer dies the swan

Though we know there are no happy endings
Still we have the nerve to carry on
Time will take our wings and all our wonder
After many a summer dies the swan

Each has his appointment in Samarra
One day I'll awake and find you gone
Give me one more sunrise to remember
After many a summer dies the swan

Speed Queen

I was busy looking forward
So I hadn't time to notice
That the night was rushing toward me
And the days were running fast
When I woke one rainy Sunday
I was facing toward the past

I was all hung up on someday
But I couldn't seem to catch up
I would find a special someone
But the sweetness wouldn't last
When I woke one rainy Sunday
I was facing toward the past

I was hungry and ambitious
Always longing for the spotlight
Busy scheming, dreaming, speeding
So I couldn't stop to see
That the one that I was beating
In my crazy race was me

I was flying toward the future
Till I finally stopped for breath
And the only one applauding
Was my lover Lady Death

The Rope

Try cutting your wrists — they will bind them up
And give you a quick transfusion
You jump off a bridge and they fish you out
There's always some damn intrusion
I won't go on! I cannot cope!
To end it all I choose the rope!

You swallow some pills but before you're gone
Their stomach pumps start in pumping
Climb out on a ledge and they'll grab you back
Before you've quite finished jumping
The rope is swift, the rope is sure
For all my ills the rope's the cure

A man may live his life alone
None share his debts and dangers
But when he's had enough he gets
Advice from perfect strangers

A pistol you say, that's the way to go
You smile as you clean and oil it
But you can be sure as you take your aim
Some ass will rush in and spoil it
If you're a chap who wants to swing
It never fails, the rope's the thing

Only Why No More

Only why no more
Sometimes never
Then beginning
Slowly something
Almost meaning
Love

Always lost at last
Sometimes quickly
Hold me, hug me
Almost reaching
Nearly home now
Cry

Only now for just a moment
Only just perhaps a meaning
Why no more
Why no more

Almost never known
Always ending
Eyes escaping
Sky returning
So long stranger
Only why no more

Beginning again
Anyway
Sometime

Cri de Cœur

(from the French of Jacques Prévert)

It's not just my voice that is singing
There are voices from the past
There is the sound of church-bells ringing
And some dreams that didn't last
There are the desperate and the gay
The siren song of yesterday
The voice of all my youthful follies
And the one that got away

There is the voice of Sister Sorrow
And the voice of fleeting joy
There is the voice of some tomorrow
That this moment may destroy
There is a fugitive who drowns
A little girl in Mother's gowns
The voice of one more fallen sparrow
That's been broken by this town

And always, always when I'm singing
That bird sings along with me
Although in pain its notes are ringing
In the face of destiny
If I could tell you all it sings
About the winters and the springs
When I was hungry and tormented
By misfortune's wicked stings

But I'd do better to forget it
For that song's no longer mine
I'm going on to something sweeter
Than that shabby Auld Lang Syne
Don't want to suffer any more
I'm gonna get up off the floor
Although my dearest friend Miss Fortune
Says 'I've heard that song before'

18

I'm going to wipe away my teardrops
I won't advertise my pain
'Cause all my two-a-penny troubles
Aren't enough to stop the train
Right now I'm on my way to Spain
Through all the sunsets and the rain
And if this planet doesn't suit me
I'm not coming here again

And if the living dead officials
At the customs stop me there
Just let them vandalise my baggage
I've got nothing to declare
Love may be on another train
But we are sure to meet again
For just like me love is a wanderer
And we're sure to meet again

Unlit Room

I'm in an unlit room
In an unmade bed
Feelin' like I'm almost drowned
I'm just an unknown bird
In an unkind town
Wishin' I was outward bound
I'm the unsung hero
Of an unwritten romance
That never did get off the ground
I'm in an unlit room
In an unreal world
Feelin' like I'm almost drowned
Oh baby
Take me to the lost and found

A Handful of Dust

Just a handful of dust
That is all we are
And we've come from a place
In the space between the stars

So a scientist said
In the paper today
And it stays in my mind
As I see the way we play

For when you seem to be so near
The fickle moment flies
And when I try to see you clear
The dust gets in my eyes

It's so hard to contain
All our anger and lust
But what can you expect
From a handful of dust

We've blown around like thistledown
Just rootless, faithless fools
Still in a straying ray of light
This dust can shine like jewels

There is one thing at least
We can cling to and trust
It's the music that springs
From a handful of dust

CHAOS AND COMEDY

Is the Common Man Too Common?

I

Is the common man too common?
Is the common man too crass?
Though we're mass-producing culture
Is it wasted on the mass?

Is the common man too tired
To enjoy an Ibsen play?
Would he rather watch a stripper
Than the Moshief ballet?

Does he miss the point of Kafka?
Has the common man a soul?
Will he cheer for André Previn
Like he does for rock and roll?

We have played him chamber music
But he never cried *encore*
We have taken him to lectures
But you should have heard him snore
And he thinks the plays of Beckett
Are a paralysing bore

II

Is the common man too common?
Will his taste improve with time?
If he reads the works of Plato
Will he give up sex and crime?

Is the common man too basic
For an art that isn't pop?
When he sees a Bergman movie
Does he wish that it would stop?

Does he opt for television?
Can we wean him from the screen?
Does his intellect stop growing
At the age of seventeen?

Is the common man perceptive?
Is the common man aware?
There is evidence around us
That he's vulgar, dull and square
And what's even more annoying
He just doesn't seem to care

Lost Lovers

Have you seen them in a restaurant
Photogenic couple turning grey
Each inside a separate sealed-off world
Sitting there without a word to say?

Wonder if they do it any more
Could it go that way with you and me?
Isn't there a way to beat that rap?
Isn't there a way to get home free?

Have you seen them in their house of glass
Alcoholic glow-worms in their eyes?
Anger gives them just the edge they need
Cutting their old sweetheart down to size

If I stay with you another year
Will we start to fall into that trap?
Dining out without a game to play
Isn't there a way to beat that rap?

Have you seen them in their Gucci shoes
Tapping out a message of despair
Run-arounds out shopping for a dream?
Could we ever grow so sad and square?

Oh my love, I'll miss you if you go
I can feel the ice begin to crack
Once I had a friend who made me laugh
Isn't there a way to get him back?

Between Chaos and Comedy

At Christmas-time we hit the road to visit friends in Wales
Indulge in media overload and acid fairy tales
With Emerald City on TV and Pink Floyd on the tape
Each friend and lover truly sees the world's in funny shape

Playing games with our emotions
Writing lyrics, crossing oceans
Between chaos and comedy

Flying off and then returning
Strumming tunes while Rome is burning
We're all part of one family

Looking into your eyes
All I see is night
Fighting off the furies
Angry at the light

Feeling with our eyes and fingers
Somehow sadness always lingers
At the edge of the comedy

Science fiction thrills us
What if it's the truth?
Sometimes panic fills us
What comes after youth?

Rolling down the lane forever
Seeing visions, being clever
Always chasing the mystery
Falling back into history
Between chaos and comedy

Love Is the Rainbow

Passion is purple, envy is green
Sorrow is heavy, kindness is clean
Anger is yellow and grief is grey
Love is the rainbow day after day

Love is the rainbow, fire and ice
Love is a vision cowards call vice
Pleasure is pinkish and fear is blue
Love is a peacock laughing at you

Love is all colours, ruby and gold
Acid and honey, wide-eyed and old
Love is a killer and love is gay
Love is the rainbow day after day

Hello Suckers!

Just look around at the London scene
What are we doing in it?
As P. T. Barnum used to say
'There's one born every minute'

Hello suckers
What are you doing here?
Did you come in lookin'
For a shoulder you can cry on
Or just a bitter beer?

Hello sucker
What do you do for kicks?
Do you do a line of coke
Or drown your dreams in whisky?
Do you know all the tricks?

Did you come in hunting with hungry eyes
For eyes that answer back
Are you a little empty?
Is that your trouble Jack?

Hello suckers
Here's what I'm gonna do
I'll show you all my stars and scars
My secrets and my sorrows
My heroes and my nights of blue
I'll flash my soul for you
'Cause I'm a sucker too

I can't resist a con man
I fall for all the fuckers
And when I pass a mirror
I whisper 'Hello sucker!'

Kings of Rock and Roll

Here we are the Kings of Rock and Roll
They say our fame will never fade
Looking back it's been a long, hard climb
But finally we made the grade
Now we'd like to tell it like it was
About the music that we played

I
We played everything
From Folk Rock to Punk Rock
Joke Rock to Junk Rock
Acid Rock to Jazz Rock
Road House, Razzmatazz Rock

High Rock and Low Rock
Whisky-a-Gogo Rock
Country Rock and Dumb Rock
Sexy Rock and Come Rock

The agents, they went into a trance
They shook their heads and said
'The kids can't dance to it'

II
So we started playing
Pow Rock and Zap Rock
Sick Rock and Clap Rock
Savage Rock and Slum Rock
Bristol Rock and Bum Rock

Horror Rock and Trash Rock
Double D and Hash Rock
Mendelssohn and Liszt Rock
Sado-Masochist Rock

The agents wouldn't take a chance
They shook their heads and said
'The kids can't dance to it'

III

So we started playing
Black Rock and White Rock
Far Outa Sight Rock
Mock Rock and Jock Rock
Sometimes it was Schlock Rock

Avant Garde and Mass Rock
Lower Middle Class Rock
Garbage Rock and Gas Rock
Shove it up your Ass Rock
Till we got right down to Bone Rock
And finally played our own Rock

The agents, they went into a trance
They stamped their feet and said
'We'll take a chance
Here's an advance
The kids can dance to it'

White Nightmare

White apple on a white plate
White fire in a white grate
White table and a white chair
White nightmare

White picture on a white wall
White carpet down a white hall
White bodies on a white bed
Overfed

Everywhere, always noonday bright
Nothing is dark, not even night
Everything clean
Everything white

White people in their white room
Lovemaking in a white tomb
White pillows for their white hair
White nightmare

White playground for a white race
No shadows in this white place
No hiding from the white glare
White nightmare

Do a Dance for Daddy

Do a dance for Daddy, make your Daddy smile
Be his little angel
Remember you're on trial
Mummy's competition, Mummy brings you down
When you're up there shining
She always wears a frown

Do a dance for Daddy. Bend and dip and whirl
You've got all that talent
'Cause you're Daddy's girl
Daddy is your hero, witty and superb
With a sign upon his door
That reads 'Do not disturb'

Look your best for Daddy
Pass your test for Daddy
Stand up tall for Daddy
Do it all for Daddy

Some day when you're older you will find romance
Someone just like Daddy
Will whistle and you'll dance
You'll recall that music when you're on the shelf
You danced for all the Daddies
But you never found yourself

Paint your eyes for Daddy
Win a prize for Daddy
Swim to France for Daddy
Do your dance for Daddy

The Past Is a Foreign Country

Today is as grey as ashes
And tomorrow hasn't a prayer
The past is a foreign country
And they do things different there

The past smells of spice and polish
And the sun shines every day
Its glory can burn forever
And it scars you as you play

Our dreams are taken from us
And memory's a sweet disease
That clouds the mind
We feed on our illusions
Where everyone was beautiful
And brave and kind

The past is a magic garden
Set behind a wall of years
Where the boys wear swords of laughter
And the girls weep sugar tears

You mourn for your missed connections
As the seasons spin too fast
You only remember the sunshine days
In the country of the past

The Heart of Darkness

The darkness which clings
To everyone's heart
Is the door to the mystery
The gateway of dreams
Two twilight figures
The shadow and the echo
Step into our visions
And twist all our schemes

And we've done it all
And we are possessed
By the snakes that breed
In the raven's nest

And the fairy tales
On a dusty shelf
Are the only clues
To the buried self

Haunted by dreams from our misty beginnings
We tangle our lovings and heap up our hates
Walking through minefields we dare not discover
That spooks in the closet are sealing our fate

And the shadow's song
And the echo's eyes
Weave a spider's web
Of seductive lies

There's a sweet perfume
On their poisoned breath
As they drag the Prince
Down the road to death

And the only clues to the buried self
Are the fairy tales on a dusty shelf

The Three Biggest Lies

The world is full of wicked liars
You can't take anybody's word
I'm gonna stand right here and tell you
The biggest lies I ever heard

'I don't need money to be happy'
'I'm proud I'm Jewish that's the truth'
'Just let me do it for a minute'
We all heard that one in our youth

I've known some great prevaricators
Those dudes can look you in the eyes
And tell you every kind of whopper
But these three gems still take the prize

'I don't need money to be happy'
'I'm proud I'm Jewish that's the truth'
'Just let me do it for a minute'
We all heard that one in our youth

The lovers con you sweet and easy
They drive you dizzy with their sighs
It's such a pleasure to believe them
And so you swallow all their lies

'I don't need money to be happy'
'I'm proud I'm Jewish that's the truth'
'Just let me do it for a minute'
We all heard that one in our youth

We hear the politicians promise
And wonder where they got the nerve
But we're just cursing our reflection
We get the leaders we deserve

'I don't need money to be happy'
'I'm proud I'm Jewish that's the truth'
'Just let me do it for a minute'
We all heard that one in our youth

We know that Jesus was a goodie
'Cause he gave everything away
He helped the poor and healed the cripples
But didn't someone hear him say —

'I don't need money to be happy'
'I'm proud I'm Jewish that's the truth'
'Just let me touch it for a minute'
We all heard that one in our youth

OLD FRIENDS

Actors

Actors are wonderful people
They're charming and talented too
Their law is the law of the jungle
They really belong in a zoo

Actors are simply delightful
They give all they have to their art
Don't say that they're vicious and spiteful
They're really just children at heart

Actors are given to whoring
It says in a book I once read
But what makes them really so boring is
They tell you about it in bed

Actors have voices like thunder
And oceans and oceans of gall
Right now I'm beginning to wonder
If actors are people at all

This song that I'm trying to sing you
Is one that I've worked on for years
I've doted on one or two actors
Our dalliance ended in tears

And after each fine careless rapture
I'd work on a verse in distress
Each time I'd endeavour to capture
The quality actors possess

Actors make terrible lovers
They're faithless, perverse and no good
And would I be caught in their spotlight
You bet your left tittie I would

The Ballad of Yesterday's Idol

Don't you know that boy?
Have you forgotten his name?
He was yesterday's idol
He was the darling of fame

How the crowds used to chase him
When that boy was tops
When he made an appearance
They had to call the cops

Yes, it's really him
He's lookin' down on his luck
He was yesterday's idol
But then the needle got stuck

They'd be tearing his clothes off
How the kids would scream
Now he sits in the shadows
Like a forgotten dream

Went to bed one night
He was the darling of fame
When he woke in the morning
No one remembered his name

That's the way it goes
It can happen that fast
When you're yesterday's idol
And your future has passed

Spite Song

I

What has she got that I haven't got?
How come she scores all those hits?
What has she got that gets them so hot?
Is it the size of her tits?

What turns you on? Her baby blue eyes?
Is it the way that she walks?
How can you sit not minding a bit
When she talks and she talks and she talks?

She waddles and she wiggles
Those forty-two-inch hips
You know she's into bondage
And owns some lovely whips

Stylish she ain't, but sexy she is
All of you studs can't be wrong
What can I do while she's playing with you
But let off steam in a song?

II

What has she got that I haven't got?
Surely it isn't her mind?
No one can stall her total recall
After she's wined and she's dined

I've seen two husbands wither and die
I've dried her crocodile tears
Sharing her beaux, her joys and her woes
I've been her buddy for years

She isn't very subtle
She isn't very smart
Beneath her iron girdle
There beats no golden heart

I shouldn't knock the lady at all
You'll only think I'm two-faced
But I can't say she's really okay
'Cause I don't admire your taste

What makes you hurry, wagging your tail
After that silly old moo?
What has she got that I haven't got?
Well, for a start, she's got you

How Come?

How come she ever lost
All the hope she never had?
What was it that she wanted from the start?
How come she ever cried
For the dreams she never tried
And couldn't learn the secrets of the heart?

She longs to go back
To where she's never been
The way that she plays
She's never gonna win

How come she can't stay home
And can never be alone
With nightmares that she's never gonna face
How come she's killing time
With no reason and no rhyme
It's sad the way her beauty goes to waste

She longs to go back
To where she's never been
The way that she plays
She's never gonna win
She's fragile as an angel made of snow
How come she hugs the thorns and can't let go?
And how come
I love her so?

Christmas Song

Dear Father Christmas, at this season of the year
My heart is growing heavy, I'm running low on cheer
But I am not requesting a special treat for me
I do not long for sweeties or a stocking or a tree
I do not ask for presents wrapped upon that festal day
But there's one little package that I wish you'd take away
Should you stumble down the chimney of my simple one-
    room flat
There is something on the sofa that is larger than a cat
It's my dear old friend George Osborne who just came to
    stay three days
And if you'd remove his carcass I'd forever sing your praise

'Cause you can't chuck consumptives out at Christmas
You can't simply dump them in the snow
Though their cough may irritate you
You know you're gonna hate yourself
If you up and tell the sweaty brute to go

Now George has many qualities endearing to us all
But when he's been around a week his presence starts to pall
He is well up on the classics and he's musical as well
But his socks are stiff as cardboard and they've got the foulest
    smell
He says that he'll be moving when a certain cheque arrives
If he isn't on my sofa he's seducing local wives
About his epic boozing many scribes have had their say
He's a legend in his lifetime and it's me that's got to pay
His habits are disgusting so the flat looks like a slum
He's eaten all my lamb chops and the Christmas pud from
    Mum

But you can't chuck consumptives out at Christmas
You can't simply dump them in the snow
Though their cough may irritate you
You know you're gonna hate yourself
If you up and tell the sweaty brute to go

He's gotten so obese no one can pass him on the stairs
The sofa's started sagging and he's broken all my chairs
He hawks and spits and wheezes so he drives me up the
 wall
If you don't come and get him I'll be sleeping in the hall
I try to bed a bird but he upsets the apple-cart
I'd ask him when he's leaving but I haven't got the heart
He's a person-non-fucking-grata to his kith and all his kin
Still I'm sure you'll find some sucker who will take the
 bleeder in
I know the Christmas spirit calls for love and charity
But I would sing hosannas if you'd take this cross from me

'Cause you can't kick the sick around at Christmas
Or else you'll be under Scrooge's curse
The entire project's out
'Cause if word should get about
You know that his replacement will be worse
You'll get an actor
You know that his replacement will be worse

The Eros Hotel

Let's go up to the Eros Hotel
And write some love songs on the sheets
We'll climb the dusty carpet stairs
That smell of hurried love affairs
Old victories and defeats

There's a bar in the Eros Hotel
It's like a party all the time
That's where you meet the unicorn
The young man with the golden horn
They all know how to rhyme

I've never been alone with you
I don't know how good we would be
And if we should collaborate
Would the music of you fit the lyric of me?

Let's go up to the Eros Hotel
And write some love songs on the sheets
The sheets are worn as soft as sin
From all the loves that might have been
The sweet sonatas of the skin at dawn
At the Eros Hotel

Dorian Gray (*for Hugo*)

Everyone calls you Dorian Gray
What is the price you're expected to pay?
All fatal beauty gets eaten away
How have you ransomed it Dorian Gray?

Where is the painting that follows your fall
Sweating away on some cobwebby wall?
Does it reproach you for smoking the weed
Rocking and rolling and swallowing speed?

Everyone wants you Dorian Gray
Climb on your motor-bike, gallop away
You'll be invaded by ants if you stay
What are you playing at Dorian Gray?

Reading your poetry there in that room
Visions like fireflies caught in a tomb
Who is the master that you must obey?
Where are you going now Dorian Gray?

How did that pale Victorian face
Gaze upon astronauts walking in space?
No sign of ageing, no whiff of decay
How does your portrait look Dorian Gray?

Jaybird

Jaybird, you took me flying
Jaybird, you showed me sights
You taught me new dance steps, neurotic romance steps
And mixed up my days and nights

Thank you, high flying Jaybird
You taught me all of my style
You gave me a hard time but showed me a good time
The message was in your smile

Jaybird, you'll never leave me
What would I ever do
If lightning should strike you? There's nobody like you
Hey Jaybird, I'd be so blue
In a nest without you

Talking Big Dreams

Remember when we'd sit around
Talking big dreams
We'd be kings of Rock and Roll
We had big dreams

We would never admit we were frightened
That the world was a big scary place
And the way that the spotlight could change us
Was something we never did face

We were heading in different directions
So the group busted up in the end
When I heard that you'd done a rock opera
I was glad 'cause you once was my friend

Well I did pretty good singing country
And got into production as well
And I'm writing commercials for cat-food
And I may not be great but I sell

Now I've paid for the farm with my music
Got some horses and tennis courts too
And I read in the *Melody Maker*
About all my old buddies like you

There were friends we just couldn't take with us
There were lovers we lost on the way
And we've stayed out of touch for a long time
And we meet and there's not much to say

So we've been where we thought we were going
Which is better than missing the bus
But it gives me the blues to remember
Those two heroes who used to be us

A Brontosaurus Named Bert

I
I had a brontosaurus
Before the world grew up
We danced among the daisies
On honey we would sup

I had a brontosaurus
I used to call him Bert
We never thought of washing
There wasn't any dirt

What times we had
That brute and I
We owned the earth
And all the sky

When everything was early
And life was sweet and slow
I had a brontosaurus
A million years ago

II
I had a brontosaurus
Before the world went mad
All day we played together
And we were never sad

I always will remember
Our prehistoric fun
Before things got so crowded
And Bertie had to run

What times we had
I felt no fear
That my dear pet
Would disappear

We danced among the daisies
On honey we would sup
I loved a brontosaurus
Before the world grew up

Second-hand Experience (*for Richard*)

Knowing you so little
I feel I know you well
Maybe I've run into you
On some street in hell
Maybe you're my brother
Stolen long ago
That's the way the script would read
If I produced the show

Second-hand experience
Richard, that's our life
Movies for a mother
Movies for a wife

Second-hand experience
Coloured all my youth
People kept suggesting
That I'd miss the truth

I found it at the movies
The drug I'd always craved
So what if I'm addicted
I'd rather not be saved

I don't mind reality
Every now and then
But a really good scene
Never runs again

I'd prefer to live my life
Down in Lotus land
Movie-loving brother
Take my coward's hand

Lennie

The ones who wrote about you never knew you
The ones who knew you didn't write
So many crippled egos living through you
Now everyone can take a bite

You made the people laugh by talking dirty
When everyone was oh so clean
Then one day everybody stopped pretending
And now we all know what you mean

Your image fills the theatres and the movies
And everybody thinks you're great
The children and the lovers and the mothers
All want a share in your estate

Too bad you didn't know when you were living
And you just couldn't get a break
That dead you'd be the biggest thing in showbiz
What kind of sick joke does that make?

I haven't read the latest book about you
They never seem to shed much light
The ones who wrote about you never knew you
The ones who knew you didn't write

Crazy Sundays

The crazy Sundays come and go
The globe is spinning fast
We meet again to lose ourselves
With darkness falling fast

We've been to parties up and down
From Hampstead to the Grove
Been crucified by butterflies
And tantalised by love

The ashtrays fill, the glasses spill
The clown and killer flirt
They scratch the itching sore of lust
And wish that it would hurt

It's fine to see professionals
Play hide and seek with pain
But in the end it's you and me
And back to bed again

The pictures on the ceiling dance
The music echoes on
You never let me fall asleep
Till all the stars are gone

I am not in my perfect mind
I have been much abused
I will not swear these are my hands
My senses are confused

So be not grieved by words of mine
For sure I am your friend
And I'd be more than sad to see
Our crazy Sundays end

TRUE CONFESSIONS

In Another Country

I was living easy
On the edge of crime
In another country
In another time

It was just a party
Where we laid it down
In another language
In another town

There was crazy music
Till the crack of dawn
He was sweet and evil
How we carried on!

I was still a stranger
On a foreign shore
Every day was different
Every night was more

Why should I be sorry
For that long lost year
In another country
Far away from here?

Do you smell his shadow
On your clean white bed?
But that's ancient history
And the man is dead

That was in another country
And the man is dead

If Wishes Were Horses

If wishes were horses
Beggars would ride
And I'd always keep you
Here at my side

If peanuts were diamonds
And kittens had wings
I'd give you a kingdom
Without any strings

If I were an angel
You'd be a saint
And wishing would help us
To be what we ain't

You may be a beggar
But you're what I crave
Though we won't be happy
This side of the grave

Just put your arms round me
Help me to hide
We'll dream we've got horses
Beggars can ride

The Argument

All we did was argue
All we did was yell
Any day at our house
Was any day in hell
When they died I never cried
I couldn't shed a tear
But in my head I try to win
The case they'll never hear

They said that I was impudent
And lazy and incompetent
So now I'll never rest content
'Cause I can't win the argument

They made me feel like nothing
They made me feel so small
The funny love they gave me
Was worse than none at all
Now I'm grown and on my own
I can't forget their words
They twitter in my tired mind
Like flocks of angry birds

Though I present my evidence
Their ghosts aren't easy to convince
They'll never let me rest content
'Cause I can't win the argument

Spirit of '76

Ain't puttin' socialism down 'cause nothin' could be finer
But anything I'd do or say would be a crime in China

The love I make, the dope I take would strictly be
  forbidden
I'd have to keep my doubts and dreams and all my
  laughter hidden

> Up at eleven and breakfast in bed
> Doesn't seem right when at heart I'm a Red
> Got to get going but what shall I wear?
> Dreaming of someone while combing my hair
> Scribbling lyrics makes hours race by
> Later there's music and everyone's high
> Sometimes I cry for the milk that's been spilt
> Mostly I'm happy though loaded with guilt

I did admire Chairman Mao and Castro was my hero
But when it comes to cutting cane I know I'd get a zero

I sing about the strains of life, the major and the minor
But anything I'd ever sing would be a crime in China

And the Birds Refuse to Shine

Then kiss me goodnight this morning
If your madness matches mine
I'll stay till the sun stops singing
And the birds refuse to shine

I'm yours till the early warning
And we're gonna do just fine
Till banners have lost their spangles
And the birds refuse to shine

Till the grass runs out
And the mountains move
If I'm by your side
You can call it love
But if you should say
That my poems were lies
Then you've never seen
Through my X-ray eyes

I'm yours till the sun stops singing
Till the darkness wins the war
When Frankenstein loves his monster
It won't matter any more

I'm yours till the floor stops swinging
If your madness matches mine
I'll stay till the sun stops singing
And the birds refuse to shine

With All My Hats

I love you with all my heart
And with all my hats
I love you with both my hands
And my Siamese cats
I love you with all my books
And my two big toes
I love you with both my eyes
And my shiny nose

I hope you find some room for these
Small tokens of my affection
I've also got a hive of bees
And a beautiful sky collection

I love you with all my heart
And my records too
I want you with all my words
And the colour blue
Please take all the songs I make
Or they'll fall apart
I love you with all my hats
And with all my heart

Jaywalkin'

I like to sleep all day and play around all night
I always cross the street against the traffic-light
I'm always ready to upset the status quo
When it says green I stop. When it says red I go

Jaywalkin', travellin' against the lights
Jaywalkin', mixin' up days and nights

I'm always getting hooked on someone else's high
I'm always getting caught without an alibi
If you're in love with me don't ever let it show
When it says green I stop, when it says red I go

Jaywalkin', breakin' up all the rules
Jaywalkin', takin' the road for fools

Won't ever do a thing because it's good for me
I got to be so bad to show myself I'm free
If it's a witch's brew just watch me drain the cup
I guess the answer is I'm scared of growing up

Jaywalkin', goin' on crazy flights
Jaywalkin', travellin' against the lights
Jaywalkin'

Swan Song

I had a little talent
I used it very well
I took it out to dinner
And fed it crème caramel

I bought it Persian incense
And watered it with wine
I had a funny feeling
It wasn't really mine

I had a little talent
It made me very proud
To do some hocus-pocus
And please a tiny crowd

It warmed me like a mantle
I couldn't see or touch
It whispered in the darkness
And never asked for much

I took my talent walking
One bright and windy day
And while my head was turning
It flew away

Find Me in Bed

You can find me in bed if you want me
If you want me that's where I will be
With the ghosts that continue to haunt me
And a nice cup of peppermint tea

You can find me in bed if you want me
In my bed where I choose to abide
I'll accept any favours you grant me
If you want me lie down by my side

Slide down the path of dreams with me
Into the sea of night
Its velvet tides will hide us from
The torment of the light

I'll be here lying back on the pillows
Staring out at the black marble sky
Where the moon hides her face in the willows
And the wind sings of danger on high

You must know I'll be happy to have you
For the poems that are locked in your head
If you're looking for someone to save you
And you want me you'll find me in bed